The Grace of Getting Up

Stories and Words of Encouragement for the Weary, Christ-Following Momma

Crystal Fulmer, EdM

WESTBOW
PRESS®
A DIVISION OF THOMAS NELSON
& ZONDERVAN

WestBow Press books may be ordered through booksellers or by contacting:

WestBow Press
A Division of Thomas Nelson & Zondervan
1663 Liberty Drive
Bloomington, IN 47403
www.westbowpress.com
844-714-3454

Scripture quotations marked ESV are taken from The Holy Bible, English Standard Version® (ESV®), Copyright © 2001 by Crossway, a publishing ministry of Good News Publishers. All rights reserved.

ISBN: 978-1-6642-9663-3 (sc)
ISBN: 978-1-6642-9664-0 (hc)
ISBN: 978-1-6642-9665-7 (e)

Library of Congress Control Number: 2023906067

Print information available on the last page.

WestBow Press rev. date: 04/17/2023

Artwork on outside cover around title: Ella (age 11)
Adoption Photo: Scott Durbin, Thousand Words Photography, Newnan, GA

To Ryan, a faithful man of God and wonderful husband who has truly honored his marriage vows over the past nineteen years, in sickness and in health.

To my babies, the six reasons God has given me to get up on the rough days when I need some tangible motivation.

To all four of my children's grandparents, our parents. We've had our tense moments and we've mostly been miles apart. However, you've not only supported us but also laid the groundwork for generational cycle breaking. We have carried on that torch in the lives of our kids.

To my second father, Mark, a beloved dad to two wonderful biological kids and a spiritual one to so many. I know you are singing with the angels in the presence of Jesus. Thank you for being proud of me and saving my life.

To K, the "tummy" Mommy and first love of my three bonus babes' lives. You are gone but not forgotten. I so wish we could have met. Thank you for choosing life.

To Micah Jude Fulmer, your short life changed mine for the better.

To my precious Heavenly Father, I am the apple of His eye.

I love you all.

Introduction

Just a few days ago, during our daily Bible time (which we absolutely *do not* accomplish daily), my eleven-year-old daughter was guided by our curriculum to read Proverbs 31 aloud.

My stomach dropped.

I've never really been a fan of that chapter.

Now I know that sounds flaky. I'm a Christian. I believe unequivocally that the Bible is the inspired Word of God, and there's a reason that this seemingly unrealistic wife of noble character is celebrated in scripture. This has always confounded me, as scripture is so gracious with our weaknesses.

One of my life verses is 1 Corinthians 1:27 (ESV). "But God chose what is foolish in the world to shame the wise; God chose what is weak in the world to shame the strong."

That's more along my line of thinking. Give me my chaotic, *tired,* messy, totally untrendy, trauma-laced, emotional roller-coaster life and I will use the fire out of it to His glory!

But another to-do list? No thanks.

Let me pause here in case these verses are a bit unfamiliar to you. Trust me: I'm far from having them memorized.

> An excellent wife who can find?
> She is far more precious than jewels.
> The heart of her husband trusts in her,
> and he will have no lack of gain.
> She does him good, and not harm,
> all the days of her life.
> She seeks wool and flax,
> and works with willing hands.
> She is like the ships of the merchant;
> she brings her food from afar.
> She rises while it is yet night
> and provides food for her household
> and portions for her maidens.
> She considers a field and buys it;
> with the fruit of her hands she plants a vineyard.
> She dresses herself with strength
> and makes her arms strong.
> She perceives that her merchandise is profitable.
> Her lamp does not go out at night.
> She puts her hands to the distaff,
> and her hands hold the spindle.
> She opens her hand to the poor
> and reaches out her hands to the needy.
> She is not afraid of snow for her household,
> for all her household are clothed in scarlet.

She makes bed coverings for herself;
her clothing is fine linen and purple.
Her husband is known in the gates
when he sits among the elders of the land.
She makes linen garments and sells them;
she delivers sashes to the merchant.
Strength and dignity are her clothing,
and she laughs at the time to come.
She opens her mouth with wisdom,
and the teaching of kindness is on her tongue.
She looks well to the ways of her household
and does not eat the bread of idleness.
Her children rise up and call her blessed;
her husband also, and he praises her:
"Many women have done excellently,
but you surpass them all."
Charm is deceitful, and beauty is vain,
but a woman who fears the Lord is to be praised.
Give her of the fruit of her hands,
and let her works praise her in the gates.
(Proverbs 31:10–31 ESV)[1]

Imagine how shocked I was when, at the end of my daughter's reading, she looked at me lovingly and said, "Thank you, Mom."

"You're welcome, honey. I know you still struggle with reading aloud, but I love it when you do."

---

[1] The Holy Bible, ESV Study, Crossway, 2008.

"No, Mom. That's not what I mean. Thank you for being like her."

For a struggling reader, my daughter read between those lines like a pro. I am convinced that in that moment, the Holy Spirit led her to see something in that passage that I had never seen.

After a normal day of fighting my anxiety/depression combo and homeschooling six kids (each with their own deep little human struggles), I'm lucky if I keep my "lamp" on past 2:30 p.m. And I *definitely* do not have the energy to go out and socialize with others or run my own side hustle.

To my surprise, however, my bright, beautiful girl saw the Spirit in this passage. She also saw me, for at least a brief moment, as God sees me.

I've researched Proverbs 31 a little bit and learned that this passage was never really intended to be fully attainable for one human being. Yet these attributes are blessings prayed over all women in celebration of who we are. If you and I, dear friend, can catch a glimpse of ourselves in one or two words of this passage, we are pearl collectors. This truth makes us rich.

How rich? I guess that depends on the depth and breadth of our attributes. However, why are we comparing our wealth? In Christ, our soul is no longer impoverished. We are all on the upside of luxury.

Some of us wake up ready to learn as much about this beautiful life as we can. Others of us open our eyes one at a time, praying that Jesus has mercy on us and counting our first steps of the day as something to be memorialized. Some of us acknowledge our struggles and it significantly slows us down; others choose to ignore these wounds so that we can keep meeting an irrational, impossible expectation.

Oh, Momma. Pick one. Pride or despair? Conceit or Jealousy? We won't escape these traps 100 percent of the time on this side of glory.

But God.

He is here in our midst. We are looking to Him, believing Him that we are who He says we are.

In the chapters to follow, I'll be mentioning all kinds of mom choices and mom "types" as our culture defines them. Some of these perceptions were skewed when my mental illness had taken over, and you will, hopefully, be able to see that my negative thoughts were fueled by a cloudy mind, heart, and spirit.

Every momma—foster, adoptive, biological, or spiritual— who does her best for her kids and her family, who fails some days and has great victories others, and who seeks to be a cycle breaker and a joy bringer is worth far more than precious jewels.

Please enjoy it. Try to push through the tension and the pain that it may bring to your heart in certain moments. This book was written with *you* in mind so that *you* would know that *you* are not alone.

Part 1

My Nine-Year Journey

Chapter 1

Trauma Is Birthed

There I was. I can still remember the panic on the nurse's and midwife's faces.

Moments before, I had delivered a deceased child, one who had passed half a pregnancy ago. I had tried to mourn him, tried to grieve his loss, before his living twin brother's arrival. I had actually convinced myself that I had fully said goodbye.

That was so, so far from the truth.

Just like the miscarriage before my firstborn, OCD and anxiety had taken over my brain after that dreaded yet somewhat expected echocardiogram. That's where we heard those awful words. "Umm, let me go grab the doctor."

They had offered me medication for my anxiety, but I couldn't—wouldn't—take it. I could power through this. After all, I was a Gen Xer (born in 1982, but I don't fit in to the millennial bric-a-brac). That resourceful, independent, balanced attitude I had always tried so hard to fake was going to see me through, doggone it!

As I was lying there after thirty-six hours of labor, the nurse swallowed deeply and said, "Honey, I can't find your baby's heartbeat, so you're going to have to push. You're only eight centimeters, but we'll lose him if we try to section you."

Without saying a word, I pushed and silently prayed like I never had before. I know epidurals have become somewhat controversial, but I'm convinced that it's the only thing that kept the pain from delivering a devastating TKO. We live in a culture that questions, scrutinizes, and debates every decision that we mommas make. I'm so glad that my God, in his sovereignty, allowed me to make the choices that were best for us and would bring Him the most glory.

Just seconds later, a young, terrified, female resident brought our boy into this world while whipping the longest umbilical cord in Fulmer family history backward (three times; I counted) away from his fragile neck.

I don't think there was a dry eye in that room.

He screamed the most beautiful scream, and I held him close. We had survived something horrific, he and I.

The nurse had to leave the room for a second, but when she came back, raccoon faced from all the mascara she had lost during delivery, she spoke positively searing words. "Momma, you just saved your child's life."

Little did I know that in that room, as my womb started the long return to normal for the last time, every emotional wound I had ever experienced was laid out and exposed.

We began a nine-day NICU journey that ended with me and little Elijah at home with my husband, my toddler, and my preschooler. We were fully happy and successfully nursing and bonding.

Unfortunately, as history *is* truly repetitive, the diapers began getting drier and less full. I pumped for a time and then ceased, the same old story. My painful introversion and our multiple moves as a pastoring, ministering family had left us, ironically, with little support. As always, I thanked God for each session we'd had together. I mourned the loss of more time connected to him in that way, and I continued through motherhood and marriage the best I could.

Except that I couldn't this time. The grief, exhaustion, and spiritual/mental battle caused my whole being to deflate. The dark thoughts got darker. The crunchy, perfect mothers were at the library, church, on the internet, and the Facebook mom groups. Just as I would do as a child, I began to believe and hang on every word of the most seemingly confident, proud, loud, and "knowledge-filled" adult in the room or internet space. No loving Heavenly Father was allowed in that purely obsessive brain.

What I heard was "You sad, sorry, sleep-training, store-bought-baby-food, nonorganic, formula-feeding mom! You may love your kids more than life and enjoy every little thing about them, but alas, you are a failure. Your children are destined for nothing but death and destruction!"

Hello, depression, my new friend.

Chapter 2

The Pit of Despair

When Ryan and I first got married, we seriously debated just adopting kids and forgoing an organic family. The need was and is so great around the world. I envisioned a Haitian or Ethiopian adoption and then maybe one or two kiddos from foster care. I never felt like I had been given an overwhelming desire to bear children. I absolutely wanted to raise and nurture them. There was just never a strong desire to biologically connect. I was a teacher with a master's in education. I had worked with just about every sect of the population. I simply loved children.

However, when those around us and those we loved began to have their own biological children, it did become a desire of my heart. Nine months after a heartbreaking miscarriage that triggered my first severe bout of OCD, anxiety, and panic attacks, I became pregnant with our firstborn son.

Two years and another state later, after transitioning from

teaching and student ministry to working in a boys group home, we had our daughter. I can still recall my faithful, Christian grandfather, whom I adored, saying, "A boy and a girl. Now you can sit back and enjoy them, and I can go to Jesus." When Ella was only fifteen months old, he did just that.

When we had moved and settled, yet again, in West Virginia, we began to discuss a third child. I never thought we would do this. Looking back, I'm befuddled as to how the adoption vision had escaped us. We were now immersed in growing our own biological tribe.

When we became pregnant with our third child, we were soon informed that *they* were our third *and* fourth. Before long, we were told they were sick. A few weeks later, it was communicated to us by one of the top fetal surgeons in the nation that our twins were the 1 percent of TTTS patients that they could not surgically fix. Because of their anatomy, it was simply too dangerous. The options were to keep them alive as long as possible with certain medication (they would both most likely die eventually) or to terminate. We chose life, and a few weeks later, our sweet Micah passed.

The perfect, divine timing in his passing saved his brother's life. Elijah James Fulmer was born extremely healthy at thirty-five weeks.

I was twenty-two weeks pregnant when our sweet boy passed in my womb, which meant that Elijah and I were the gatekeepers of his lifeless body for thirteen weeks.

I remember the leading fetal specialist at Cincinnati Children's Hospital calling me from his personal cell the day that Micah died. He told me that none of this was my fault, that there was nothing I could have done to change the outcome, that there was immense hope for my living baby, and that my husband and I were a true inspiration. He also told me to call him anytime I wanted to talk or had any questions.

I have to be honest, and I might come off a bit selfish. I didn't want to be an inspiration. I wanted *both* of my baby boys.

Isn't it interesting how oftentimes the people who are the most influential in our thought patterns are the ones who say the most devastating things in times of crisis, grief, and trauma?

"You need to do everything you can to keep those babies alive."

"You would have never been able to handle four children anyway."

There were others, far removed from our inner circle, who were truly used to encourage and edify. Yet sadly, those condemning thoughts are the ones that stuck. It seems they always are.

On July 23, my daughter's third birthday and when my precious Elijah was only two months old, I checked myself into a mental hospital.

I didn't want to go on. I had thoughts of taking a bunch of pills and going on peacefully. I truly believed my children would be better off without me. I had spent months obsessing over all the things I had done wrong as a mom. Somewhere deep down, I was convinced I'd murdered my own child out of pure idiocy. I just *knew* that they needed a different mommy and that God had a made a terrible mistake choosing me.

I spent a week in that facility. I was quite blessed by my time.

I actually ministered to people there, listened to their stories, and attended my first AA meeting just to absorb the knowledge.

I remember, in particular, one nurse wrapped her arms around me when I first arrived. She said, "Sweetheart, drug-addicted mommas have perfectly healthy babies. Who gets to bring children into this world has never made sense to anyone except God."

Two weeks later, I started counseling with a fantastic Christian counselor. I also restarted medication that I had ceased prior to my second full-term pregnancy. I wish I could say that was all I needed.

Days into talk therapy, I was in another facility. Ryan had called my counselor, who contacted this place. I was physically paralyzed in my bed. I couldn't move. I couldn't rise and face another day. He didn't know what else to do.

That horrible experience was the beginning of my walk to freedom. My counselor had remembered it as a place of beauty and rest when he had worked there, but it was now far from that. I shared a room with a psychotic (and most likely demon-possessed) woman who ripped our sink out of the wall. People were nasty and vulgar. I wanted to leave. Ryan would come every day and beg them to release me. They held me for a week. A trauma within my trauma. It's just like God to make that the start of something good.

I don't know exactly what happened to my heart and mind after that experience. All I can say is that the next time I woke up in my own bed hearing the sweet little cries of my three-month-old, simultaneously wanting to vanish from this world, a strong, almost audible voice said, *"Get up."*

I did. And I have. Every day since.

Chapter 3

The Ups and Downs on an Ascending Trajectory

It would be so lovely if this chapter could be the epilogue.

I mean it would make for a short book, but a really easy life.

God hasn't allowed me that luxury though. I believe He loves me (and you) *a lot,* and He's in the business of making His kids walk desperate, burdensome, horrific roads in order to find significant joy and blessing. His discipline can be harsh, but it is so good. Also, He cries with us and holds onto us every step of the way. He's amazing.

The next three years after those hospital stays are, in some ways, a blur. My oldest child, Cohen, attended kindergarten at a truly wonderful public school down the road that first year. I subbed part time and stayed home mostly with our doll-faced three-year-old and butterball preemie. I continued with my tenderhearted therapist who became a second father to Ryan and me. I regularly attended Celebrate Recovery meetings.

My oldest had never been one to pick favorites when it came to Ryan and me. Truthfully, he'd always operated (aside for a handful of weeks in his infancy) with a trust and love for all people. However, I remember those kindergarten Mondays when he would come home from school and I would have to drive away to my grief recovery meetings. He cried for me.

It broke my heart, but I knew staying home wasn't an option. I was so incredibly emotionally frail, and I had to learn to be the best wife and mother possible for my family.

The next two years after that were full of change.

Elijah turned one in the spring, and Ryan and I spread his identical brother's ashes in the ocean that September. By the following fall, I had a small babysitting operation in my home. I was able to manage that OK for a while—until I couldn't.

By the time Elijah turned two, I had decided to homeschool. I'm not sure that all my reasons were right at the time, but I'm sure the decision was from the Lord. Cohen was so academically bright, and the loss of a fully formed baby boy gave me a new realization of the fragility of life. I never, *ever* wanted to shelter my kids, but I truly missed my big boy during the day, and it made my stomach drop to think of sending his green-eyed bubbly sister off to pre-K.

As the rest of us dove into homeschool, Ryan dove into finding a new position. He wanted to become a lead pastor.

The first church that offered him a position in the area (that could possibly grow into a lead) was where he was taking his master of divinity classes. It was incredibly kind of them, but I knew I couldn't survive this particular church's culture. It was the first time in the history of our relationship that I drew a hard line. I was never good at boundaries, and I was horrible at letting others say or do whatever they wanted around or to me. My intense emotional pain, however, had taught me that I had a voice. After all, I was daily fighting for my life. I put my foot down.

I knew he wanted to go. I knew he wanted to spend time learning from some brilliant, theologically sound men, but I also knew I couldn't have survived. My husband heard my heart, and God blessed him.

On May 1, with the help of our "second father" and my female CR mentor, my husband became pastor of Perrow Church. It was only twenty minutes away from the church where he had held his previous position as student pastor. We didn't have to start completely over. I was worried that the community of Perrow would be similar to the culture I'd seen at large that had seeped into other churches.

First of all, it wasn't. The people were and still are wonderful and "my people."

Secondly, as my husband had predicted, through the Holy Spirit we got to set the cultural tone for the church. I didn't realize how extraordinarily that would play out until we became honest and open about our past to our newfound brothers and sisters. From there, the beautiful floodgates of brokenness and vulnerability opened wide.

Unfortunately, being my sensitive self in the homeschool world was different. I loved the small public school community we had joined and knew *nothing* about homeschooling despite the fact that I spent five years of my young adult years getting a degree in how to teach children.

Also, stereotypes are there for a reason. I immediately was faced with being a modern-day, doctor-trusting, conventional mom in a somewhat vaccine-hesitant, extended-breastfeeding, organic-obsessed culture. By this point, we were making some changes in our home as well. However, for the most part, I felt so awkwardly out of place. I will forever and ever feel deep gratitude and love for the moms who made me feel welcome and comfortable in that foreign land.

One thing is for sure. Being in that group of women and humungous families every other Friday made me feel like I was due for another baby.

I actually would soon have three more of them.

Although just like everything else in my life, they didn't come naturally.

Chapter 4

Navigating True "Self" Care

What I wanted more than anything was to get off medication. There is such a stigma attached to it. So around our second year at Perrow, I made the decision to try to taper off again.

I made a friend at church who had walked a similar road as me, losing a baby late term in her pregnancy. As we were at a playdate one day, my mind was racing and I was spewing all these thoughts out to her. I know she could see my high anxiety level and my need for relief.

As she handed her months-old rainbow baby to me so that she could make his bottle, she said, "You know, Crystal, there's nothing wrong with medicine. I'm on it and I'm OK with being on it for the rest of my life. I'm not saying you'll never get off, but I'm saying maybe you should embrace that idea at least until you can really fully heal."

She didn't know it then, but I needed that so badly. I needed someone like her, who not only had walked what I walked and had chosen medication but was also a medical professional, to say, "It's really OK."

Within a month, I was back on my meds and feeling so much better. To this day, I'm trusting God with that decision. I know he will lovingly convict or just give me a clear better choice when, or if, it's time for something new.

I'm currently working through the spiritual side of bondage and strongholds from my past. Maybe that'll do it. Maybe it won't. Maybe it all really is chemical as real as a brain tumor or chronic disease. Truly, I'm just trusting God with it, and there's so much peace in that.

What I started to learn through that decision (and others like it) is that I have to discern where the condemnation and truth come from. What I mean by that is that there will be people unknowingly used by the dark prince of his world to make me feel like a failure. There are others who unfortunately are void of any self-respect, whether in or out of the truth, who are narcissistic and see a target in my empathetic spirit.

Yes, I need to love all of my brothers and sisters in Christ, for sure. However, I don't need to surround myself with them continually, especially on days I know I'm weak and cannot stand against those forces. I need to *constantly* surround myself with people who I can encourage and who will encourage me. I believe that is why Jesus had three close friends. These men were predestined to speak His language, to connect to Him the way your best friend does to you. And these people are few and far between.

Sweet friend, hear me.

We have lived too long in the church culture simply accepting things like verbal, emotional, and spiritual abuse from others. Do we love those who speak in hurtful ways to us? Of course. We forgive them as well. However, as a group, whether they hurt us a lot or a little, we must confront boundary-crossing, narcissistic behavior with clear reminders that those things are not acceptable in the kingdom and family of God.

Too often, I've heard, "Well, that's just who he is" or "She's always been that way."

No!

They deserve better, and so do those who have been hurt by them.

Self-care really falls back into group care when you are a Christian. When we are honest with one another when we've been wounded, always encouraging, always apologizing, always forgiving, and always speaking truth in love, we are united; we are in tune with one another and with the Holy Spirit. Also, we're taking care of ourselves because we are drawing and keeping those precious boundaries we need.

Doing that has made all of the difference in our family life.

I always thought my little tribe would learn how to grow into adulthood by watching their mom and dad be "nice" to everyone.

How far from the truth.

I have drawn hard lines in the sand. I have said rough, albeit loving, words. My kids have seen me weep over words that have hurt me. They have heard me use words like "bullying" to refer to adult behavior. These people have not been vilified in our home in any way. We still speak kind words over them. The truth remains. My children are learning how to treat others and how to allow themselves to be treated. They are learning that they are God's precious jewels and that standing up for themselves isn't harsh or wrong in the least. They are being equipped, and I'm so proud of the little joy-makers and bold speakers that they are becoming.

I would argue that the American church has long lost its collective spirit of discernment. We've traded seeing the personal and spiritual "bones" of the person for valuing what they do and the individual (disconnected from sin) choices they make. This is so dangerous as God purifies His church, which He promises He's doing.

I am the chief of sinners when it comes to making judgments based on these things. I actually have a very strong spirit of discernment, a total gift from God. It was overshadowed for years by my mental state. The enemy rejoiced in this, but my Savior actually used it to unveil some painful truths about how we can view each other with shallow hearts.

Ultimately, my journey in this area has never been more for my good and God's glory than when it came to adding trauma-affected kids to our family.

Chapter 5

One Simple Decision

Our family moved to the same town as Perrow after Ryan had been pastoring there for six months or so. About a year or two into living in our new home, we began talking about foster care. I was on meds, was in counseling, and had been stable for quite some time.

I have to say that you're never the same after losing a child. Many women (like me) are deeply affected by early term miscarriages as well. These events don't trigger just grief.

From my experience, there is a deep chemical reaction that causes things to run amuck psychologically for many of us. I will never get my preloss brain or heart back unless the Lord decides to do something miraculous. I pray that He releases me. However, I also pray if this is supposed to be some sort of "thorn" that my Father chooses not to remove, that I will carry it with strength, joy, and purpose. After all, without this particular thorn, you probably wouldn't be reading this book right now.

Foster care isn't just for the strong, miraculously patient, and wealthy. It's for anyone who wants to say yes. It's for those who want to help and not just become a better parent but a better human being and witness for Christ. For those He calls, He equips.

It took a few talks and prayers for my husband to be on board with the idea. We knew we wanted more kids, but my mind, heart, and body were done with pregnancy. It terrified both of us to think what would happen if we suffered another pregnancy loss. It was as if our initial desire to adopt was a foreshadowing of future events.

Ryan slowly came around. There was a foster care agency moments down the road from us and we began to take classes.

As we began the process, many people either silently or vocally showed their disdain for our choice. First, there were lots of feelings of frustration and fear that Ryan wouldn't be able to handle this along with church responsibilities. Also, there was concern that I wouldn't be able to handle "troubled" kiddos while homeschooling. Finally, there had been a short history of foster parenting in the church that had mostly turned out badly.

The majority of people in our circle, however, were very excited and ready to help and support. Even some who had tried foster care and hadn't succeeded offered their hearts and encouragement!

Really, the one thought that kept ringing in my ears was *If not us, then who?*

As cliché as it sounds, that one question really applied to Ryan and me.

He had been a student minister for years. He knew those kids, he knew their homes, he knew their brokenness and traumas, and he ministered well.

I remember doing a long-term substitute position in a second grade class in Ohio. There, the classrooms were divided up by behavior and performance, which obviously had its benefits and downfalls. Of course, the teacher I was subbing for had the low-performing/high-behaviors class. The other second grade teacher said to me on the playground one day, "You were made for these kids. I don't know how you do it."

Our work at a chain of group homes for two years eventually took its toll on our growing family, but we loved the boys as our own and took great pride in their accomplishments and healing.

Bottom line, we weren't going into this naïve. I can look back now and tell you there was plenty we didn't know about the undertaking of bringing these children into our home. The one thing we *did* know was that God had led us through a lot of unique experiences and we had sacrificed a great deal in the process. These trials would not go to waste.

The foster classes were good and helpful. We learned a lot in some while trudging through others. We made a lot of really good connections and wise decisions about who we would be willing to take into our home as well as who would benefit from us. We had enough space for two. We opened in December 2018.

We were ready for up to two extra kiddos, between ages zero and four, any color of the rainbow, any religious background, and also preferably available for adoption.

We, as a family of five, were happy and fulfilled. We enjoyed and loved each other and found meaning and wholeness within our unit of five. This didn't mean that a child that we adopted would be "extra" or not part of the whole. In fact, they would just make the "whole" bigger. What it did mean was that until a child or children was/were legally ours, they were a ministry. They were children God had called us to love, protect, parent, and walk beside for the time of His choosing. However, they would not belong solely to us as there was still opportunity for reconciliation with biological family.

Oh, but we so hoped that the first children would be ours forever, not out of desperation but desire.

We got a lot of calls through the first few months of 2019. There were a few we had to turn down right out of the gate, and that hurt so much. There were a few to whom we said yes, but then something else had been worked out quickly through another agency and those ended up not panning out either.

Our very first call (a newborn, biracial baby girl) broke my heart and made me want to quit before we started. We brought all of Ella's old clothes down from the attic, set the Pack and Play by my side of the bed, and stayed ready to get the call that we could come see her in the local hospital.

Within twenty-four hours, we learned a family member had stepped up. She was gone. She was a little baby girl I had never met, but my heart broke all the same.

This roller coaster continued into March, when we got a call during a church prayer meeting on a Monday night.

Chapter 6

Never Really Ready

By 9 p.m. that Monday night in March, two young, exhausted social workers were at our door with a twenty-two-month-old baby girl and a three-and-a-half-year-old baby boy, the two youngest of a sibling set of five. The little girl just wanted to be held that first night, and the little boy simply wanted to move. Trying to comprehend what they had seen and experienced that day was hard on my mind, heart, and soul.

The social workers explained that they would be eligible for adoption soon, but we had already been warned not to get too excited in hearing those words. It's amazing the comebacks that the legal guardians can make, and many times judges award second, third, and fourth chances.

Most of the story, I'll leave for the kids to tell when they're older, but adoption definitely looked like the outcome from the beginning. Their biological mom had lost rights years prior. The terms of her termination stated that she was not allowed near her kids. However, their grandmother, who had adopted all five children, allowed their mom to stay with her.

It still boggles my mind how one chooses between one's child and one's grandchildren. Sadly, the elderly generation is constantly met with this decision.

In any event, this caused the removal of the children from the home.

The social workers also conveyed to us that they felt there was extra hope for these two little ones. Their older siblings, one other child and two adolescents, had been through some tough times.

This began our journey with Michelle and James. (In this book, I'll call them Michelle and James.)

James immediately seemed to become a Fulmer. People laugh when I say that, but it's true! Don't get me wrong. Those early days could be tough, especially after the "honeymoon phase" was over. His tantrums were hard sometimes, and every second his eyes were open, he was sensory seeking. His hands and body were all over everything and everyone. His speech was not understandable at all in the beginning, and his movements were very stiff.

However, there was something about that kid that made it feel like he always belonged. He was delayed quite a bit and working with him was like drawing on a blank slate. The sky was, and still is, his limit.

Michelle, on the other hand, who was so sweet and cuddly coming into our home, quickly became quite difficult to handle. Unlike her brother, she was not only extremely fluent and clear in her language skills but could comprehend quite well also.

However, she chose screaming most of the time. We struggled with figuring out what was defiance, what was trauma, and what was a little of both. She snatched, hoarded, and ingested everything she could get her hands on. Despite her precious, lovey attitude with every new person she met, she struggled with understanding and figuring out her emotions at home with us. It seemed as though relationships were very, very difficult for her.

Those early days, after the month or so of "honeymooning," were the most difficult, especially since these babies didn't even get to see their other siblings for several months. Looking back, I still struggle with shame over how poorly I handled so many things, namely their unfamiliar and constant behaviors. There was no daycare available for the kids because I didn't hold an outside job. Having to wade through my third year of homeschooling with these behaviors was altogether awful. They were confused, hurt, and their senses were overwhelmed.

I failed. A *lot*.

I was trauma informed and trained, but even when using those skills, I don't think I was frequently effective. I went from a mother who, even during the "Breakdown of 2015," was mostly kind and patient with her children to an absolutely unpredictable emotional mess.

As I scoured the internet and picked the brains of other foster parents for help, I quickly learned the sad irony of the impoverished American family.

Due to issues like poverty, drugs, and/or depression in the adults' lives, these children are most likely neglected emotionally and physically. Yet they can be overwhelmed materialistically during the holidays or when a government check comes in. They are given anything and everything that would keep them from losing their tempers and disturbing their parents' agendas or emotional issues.

I'm not sure how much of this was true for my new babies. I can say, however, that now that they were in a home that cared more about their emotions and growth, the little ones God entrusted with me were acting out because it was so opposite of anything they'd ever experienced. Also, I'll be the first to admit their behaviors were truly nothing for which I had or could have prepared myself.

In June, we began visits with siblings. Temporarily, the three older children were together in a kinship home. It was good getting to know them and understanding the dynamic of these kids. It was clear that the older kids missed the youngers terribly and were a little saddened upon hearing them call us "Mommy" and "Daddy." This wasn't our choosing, but just something both littles had started to do quite quickly.

At the beginning of the 2019–2020 school year, the three older children in the kinship home were sent to two different homes. The two older girls moved to a state home fairly close to us, and the older brother moved about two hours away.

Pretty soon after this exchange, we learned that their grandmother would be awarded visits. This was shocking to us as the case seemed very open and shut.

The visits started in a neutral spot and then transitioned to a new home she had purchased. There was a part of me that enjoyed dropping the babies off, knowing that they were connecting to their biological family and that we got a little more time with ours. However, I spent much of that time fighting back tears.

I remember one particular Sunday afternoon sitting in a restaurant across from my husband during the littles' visit. I immediately had a flashback to years earlier, sitting across from him in a crowded dining establishment in downtown Cincinnati, visibly pregnant, saying, "What are we going to do? What are we going to do if we have two severely handicapped children? What are we going to do if we lose both of them? How will we—how will I—carry on?"

Two totally different circumstances. Both ending in Jesus consistently asking me to let go.

Anxiety and grief. Two old foes that by the grace of God, I'd defeated once. I was resolved that I'd do it again.

That doesn't change the pain though.

You know, I admire foster parents who are all in it for the kids and the family. I do.

I also understand the opposite attitude of "I can't even think about foster care because I couldn't give them back."

The truth, for me, is somewhere in the middle. Despite how weary these kids made Ryan and me, we loved them, we poured into them, we planted and watered them, and we even made mistakes with them like they had always been our own. However, there was this undeniable peace that God was going to do what was best for them and us.

We just didn't know what that would look like yet.

Chapter 7

When Theology Changes but Grace Increases Even More

I have a quick scholarly lesson for you all!

In reality, this may be basic milk for many of you.

There are basically two branches of Protestant theology. One is called Arminianism and one is Calvinism or Reformed. Most of us who call ourselves Christians, without studying these branches, would probably fall somewhere between these two systems. I would venture that most American Christians have no clue what either of these two words really mean, which is actually just fine. Neither belief system really takes away from your faith or salvation.

If you believe that the Father's Son, Jesus's death, on the cross and miraculous resurrection is the bridge that has connected your sin-stained life back to God's loving-kindness and salvation, that's the meat and bones. That's it. The Gospel. Your life and how you live it will be fruit of that single belief.

However, I had grown up hearing "Calvinist" as almost an insult. I grew up in a *very* Arminian church, as did my husband.

Our home churches, in a nutshell, believe that man has absolute free will in their decision to follow Christ—in all decisions, really. They believe that Christ calls us all and that some come to Him. They believe that man didn't fully "die" at the fall of Adam, just became very ill.

As we were working at the group home, Ryan was reading a great deal and was introduced to some Calvinist authors who changed our theology completely. Calvinism (or Reformed theology) says that the Father has known since before the beginning of time what was going to happen.

Every single detail. He is fully Sovereign.

Not only that, but he predestined all things. He calls people to Him, and those whom He calls cannot resist His call. This is all for His glory. It's for a bigger story that's yet to be fully known to us but has absolutely been written. What we know is that He (including His goodness, faithfulness, love, compassion, etc.) wins in the end!

This is offensive to the flesh, yes, when we think about those whom we love who are not yet followers of His. However, it also gives us rest. Not just about our loved ones but ourselves.

Here was the big selling point for me, especially after having my second child: everything that I've done, whether it be failure, mistakes, or sin (and even the good stuff—successes, obedience, triumphs)—God has a plan for it all. And it is good!

This, as others have stated about this theology, comes over me like a warm blanket.

Therefore, although my OCD and the enemy tell me to wallow in my past junk, my Creator screams, "Stop it! I'm using it *all,* girl! Put it *down!* It's *mine!* I'm making it into something beautiful!"

This, friends, is so important. At this moment, I'm 160 pounds at a mere five foot, four. I just exercised for the first time in a month. By "exercise," I mean a few yoga poses. I'm currently eating an apple, but I've also been snacking on sweets all day that my uncle sent from the Netherlands.

God is taking my husband and me through some tough realities about how we've treated one another in our marriage, and I have some true bitterness that I didn't even know was there! Although we both love each other dearly and faithfully, there's a little temporary distance at the moment.

Also, at this very second, my seven-year-old is standing in the corner because he said a word (that's not a cuss word but sounds like one) and I've asked him repeatedly not to say it!

This is real life. This isn't the hustle or the perfect image that social media presents. My family and I are dealing with stuff and we're getting through it. Sometimes we run gleefully, but many times we're walking, and others, we're crawling at a snail's pace.

However, we have the faith and the track record to know that God's going to work all these things for our good as well.

Reformed theology continues to offer me the peace and vulnerability to say, "If I could do it over again, life would be so much different. However, the Lord has a plan for this life of mine. He's preordained all my days, and I wait patiently with joy and hope."

The unfortunate part that I've learned about Reformed theology is that many of its followers don't live in this grace, nor do they extend it to others. It's baffling to me really. It's like they recognize that they were dead and Christ made them alive again, but they're still kind of dead. They are just as set in their ways and legalistic as the Arminian church I grew up in. And so ironically, all of us, in some ways, are trying to earn the favor of a God who already loves us just as we are!

I guess we're all prone to it, aren't we? Gracelessness, legalism, judgment, etc. It's all there and very strong. The enemy is always looking to hold us in bondage, whether it's pride or despair or wealth or poverty.

I want to be free, don't you?

"Yep! That's me! The *chief* of sinners! I can't go through the first five minutes of my morning without sinning! I thank God for His grace! I thank Him that I am now a *saint*. My desire is obedience, but when I fail, I know I'm still His child, and that's all that matters."

This is the attitude that carried me through my unbearable days of grief, mental illness, raising trauma-effected foster children, and then *COVID*.

And gaining one more bonus babe.

Chapter 8

How Can We Say No?

One thing that can be said about the Reformed Christian culture in America is that they, like Catholics, feel strong that many children are considered a blessing. I've even begun to understand how the "extremists" (who, yes, exist in all branches of Christianity) believe that a wife's job truly is to be the ancient point-by-point Proverbs 31 woman that King Solomon spelled out hundreds of years before Christ. Basically, we should have as many kids as possible, raise them, teach them, cook for them, and still make plenty of time for our husbands. It's almost as if we're being told that we're raising little armies for Jesus, as if He couldn't take care of this whole sin problem all on his own.

Wait. Hasn't He already done that once?

Interestingly, when we found out we were having twins, Ryan jokingly said, "Now we can be *real* Calvinists, because you have to have at least four to make the cut, right?"

Also, in recent years, Evangelical conservative America has done something that it really likes to do: take the extreme opposite stance of the progressives.

So the liberals say we shouldn't have kids? The liberals want to tear down the family?

We'll fix this by having armies of kids!

This is a bit sad to me, because over thousands of years, we (the secular *and* religious cultures) have never learned that we are not all called to the same thing. There was never a time in the Bible where God said, "Have at least _____ children so you can receive My blessing."

Of course, children are a blessing. Of course, it is good to have precious babes and toddlers scooting and tumbling around the sanctuary and the nuclear home. They are refining us and keep us young. They're the hope of the future church. As parents, our children grow us into the men and women God wants us to be. They provide help and comfort in our old age. Most importantly, they sanctify us and help us let go of youthful selfishness.

If you're married, I recommend them—as many as you would like and that you can handle. However, please, I *beg* of you, don't do it because a huge part of our world has become antichild. Don't do it because everyone else seems to be having procedures done to prevent having their own kids. Don't do it to prove your pro-life stance. Don't do it to tease or judge those who aren't all about childbearing. Do it because it's something you've prayed about, it's your call, and it's your joy.

Also, I would implore that you consider foster care and/or adoption.

As you know by now, we didn't have four biological children. We didn't reach that religious, social status.

However, through the grace of God and His uncanny ways of bringing His family together, we have six.

Elizabeth (again, not her real name) started coming to us in February 2020 for weekend visits. She was our bonus babies' big sister and attended kindergarten one town over from us. Grandma had fought in court for nearly two years at this point, and she was reaching the end. The case was going toward what we knew would be a termination of rights and headed into adoption.

Since the beginning, the idea of Elizabeth coming out of her current placement and living with us had been discussed. However, the timing was never right. We had recently moved into a larger home and it was time to welcome her.

Our plan was to have her every weekend and spring break until the end of that school year. Then no matter what the adoption process was looking like, we were going to homeschool her with our own biological kids.

However, what happened in mid-March of 2020 is literal history.

Elizabeth did go with us on spring break, and because of COVID, she never went back to her former foster home. She finished her kindergarten year online at our house, and she became a foster child in our home under our agency.

It was only a month later, in April 2020, that we had to give her devastating news. Her grandmother had lost custody and was terminated from her care. Of course, Elizabeth knew this was likely to happen because this is why she had transitioned to our home. Still, the pain was intense and real. We held her while she shook, cried, and mourned the hope she had left of ever getting the family she always knew back again.

We kept a connection with their older sister's foster home until she decided to move into transitional living at the age of seventeen. We also got to meet her boyfriend after she transitioned and we've invited them on many of our escapades as a family. My biological kids have gained a big sister and she has gained three more younger siblings.

On March 15, 2021, we adopted all three kiddos in a court proceeding online. The day was full of pictures, a huge party, and lots of joy.

We also got to know the guardianship family of our three bonus babies' big brother, and he was present that day. He has also continued to be a huge presence in their lives.

By adoption day, our family had grown extensively. It was pretty amazing to see everything that God had done.

However, "happily ever after" is really such a naïve, far-off notion when it comes to the reality of this world. My hope is that one day the words "Well done, good and faithful servant" will be my "happily ever after." Until then, there is much work to do. Life has been joyful but so difficult since we became the Fulmer Family Eight.

Chapter 9

Rest

There're going to be a lot of people who put this book down halfway through this chapter. They're going to say, "You know what? This is too much. I can't handle this mom of six telling us it's OK to be lazy!"

Let me be straight with you. We (the late Gen Xers, millennials, and Gen Zers) are the generations that are, at some point, going to have to stop and breathe and start really breaking some cycles for the sake of our children.

Cycle breaking doesn't mean doing the exact extreme opposite of our parents or grandparents. It means that we take little steps while giving ourselves lots of grace to do better.

After sweet Elizabeth joined our crew, I knew I had already been to hell's front gate and back. When Elijah was a baby and toddler, I didn't sleep at night or relax at all for months that turned over to years because the voice of the enemy said, "You don't deserve to relax. You are a horrible human being."

I remember when the SSRI really started to change my brain (like almost a year into using it daily) and I learned how to balance quick-acting benzodiazepines (disclaimer: these can only be used with nonaddicts) with better food choices, herbs, light therapy, prayer, and the reading of God's Word. It was unbelievable. There was popping and cracking all over my body. There was this flexibility and bounciness that I had forgotten was connected to the human form. I enjoyed food, my husband, and my children, and my God again.

But I was tired.

Then add two moves, new "professions," two new kids, then three, then a *pandemic.*

I had five kids at home with me during the 2021–2022 school year. I was their mom and teacher. Our little Michelle did pre-K in the public sector. She definitely needed the separation to understand emotions and the difference between family and others.

For the two years we fostered these kids, we *never* sought respite. I knew deep down these kids were going to be ours and we needed to create that bond; handing them off to strangers just wasn't something I could sign off on.

However, their trauma was still visible, tangible, and heavy. Their grandmother, who had previously been their legal guardian, died of COVID in the middle of the pandemic. Michelle and James continued to struggle and progress in all the ways they always had. However, Elizabeth *really* struggled with her relationship with me. She, for completely understandable reasons, wanted to be my baby at six and then seven.

I, for obvious reasons, could never make this happen for her. She was six months older than Elijah and I had two of her biological baby siblings to raise as well. She couldn't restore or improve the connection that she'd had with her biological mother through her and my relationship. I would never be her first mom, and it would never be OK for me to try to take her place.

Foster and adoptive parents are human. If you're reading this and you are one, you know exactly what I mean. You can love a child who feels rejected, abandoned, jealous, and deprived to the moon and back, but there's this hole in the bottom of the cup that always leaks; it's never full. Every day, you simply love the best you can, and you wait on time to be the true healer.

I am so thankful to Jesus that Ryan's job at this time was flexible and not physically demanding. I'm so thankful that he graduated with his MDiv around the time that Elizabeth joined us.

I bottomed out. There's no other way to put it.

Every day, I made sure my kiddos got breakfast and lunch. I taught them how to put letters together to make words and how to add, take away, and do all the advanced stuff my olders were getting into. I taught them about the Revolutionary War and Civil War and all kinds of cool modern inventions. I read aloud to them the classics and we had Bible time together. I made sure they got to co-op or any extra events during the day. I made sure dishes were washed and laundry was done (not done, but ya know, they could at least dig something clean out of the pile).

Beyond that, when that clock said 2:30 p.m., I hid in my bedroom until their dad got home. Sometimes I came out for dinner (to make, help, or eat) and beyond; sometimes I didn't.

I was suffering from severe emotional exhaustion, secondary trauma, and just an overall feeling of suffocation. I couldn't sit in my own living room to watch a movie or play a game without feeling the massive amounts of jealously in the air over me.

I'm sure God was laughing at my predicament a bit. I'd carried around this "bad mom" syndrome for years. I'd find it so awkward, off-putting, and even condemning when other babies would only want their moms and my kids would happily accept either my husband or me for the most part. Now all of a sudden most of the kids wanted to feel close to me all at the same time— and I frankly didn't know what to do with myself.

This predicament I found myself in was clearly no one's fault. There was nothing I could do about the fact that I had borne three of the children living in our house and fed them for a time from my own body. There was nothing the three others could do about the fact that they were born into chaos, that their biological mom had been enduring her own deep struggles as they grew, and despite the fact that they had been adopted, there was still opportunity.

I couldn't become for them the biological mother that they had lost. I could love them unconditionally. I could discipline them and raise them in the Lord. I could give them hugs, kisses, and "I love yous" until the cows came home. However, I could never, ever, ever become their "tummy" Mommy, as we began to call her.

Elizabeth, Ryan, and I had (and still have) so many talks about who she is to us, why she was so much smarter and more loved than she truly believed she was, and why we couldn't coddle her forever.

She was not the first child in our lives who wanted a do-over. We had boys in the group home who were the same way.

I so get it. If I wanted a do-over for my first several years as a bio mom, why would I find it unusual for a kid to want his or her childhood back?

But at some point, as we told Elizabeth, we have to plant our feet firmly where God has us. We have to mourn our past, thank Him for the memories, and trust that it all will eventually make us stronger. We have to believe the good that other people say about us and understand that all the nasty we may hear in our heads is not from the Lord. When He convicts, whether through our parents, our friends, or our siblings, it is sweet, kind, and loving.

At the end of her second grade year, Elizabeth gained a stellar talk therapist who prayed with her and talked to her about Jesus. She was building confidence, enjoying time with her biological siblings when she could, and looking forward to the hope that one day she could restore a relationship with her biological mother with whom she shared a small treasure trove of sweet memories.

Then sometime in mid-May, I got a text from big sister. "Hey, Crystal. I'm so sorry. I don't know how to tell the kids. Mom died last night."

Chapter 10

Death

Some of us meet death early—a parent, grandparent, aunt, uncle, or cousin. Maybe it's even the tragic death of a kid in our class at school.

Others of us, however, live in ignorant bliss for years until the floodgates open. In the years of 2020–2021, I lost my grandmother and my counselor who was a fatherly mentor to me. My bonus babies lost their grandmother in May 2021 and their mother in May 2022.

Like I said in the previous chapter, the whole pandemic was about emotional survival for me. I was not depressed or terribly anxious. I took my medication, went to the doctor, and though I gained weight (like most of the country), I didn't eat or drink myself into oblivion. I even kept up with some walking, yoga, and mild aerobics. Because I'm a bit neuro diverse, I wasn't reading my Bible much, but I was listening to it daily. And yeah, I was enjoying some true crime docs, podcasts, and novels for my own release.

I also was allowing my husband to step in a lot when he was home. The incessant needs of our instant family were hard for me to bear twenty-four hours a day/seven days a week. All my emotions were drained.

Despite his stepping in, we still felt very balanced and in tune as a couple. He pastors a smaller church, so his energy level is still quite high when he comes home. Also, as it is with most men, he desires to see a task begun and finished in a short amount of time (not always possible when God works in church ministry), so he had learned to take joy and pride in dishes and dinner.

Then these babies' tummy Mommy died, and I honestly thought, *I have to wake up. I have to be strong. I have to be present.*

Ultimately, my babies' momma was able to have a small service and we took the kids before the guests arrived. Elizabeth humbled and blessed me by asking me to set the note she had written and picture she had drawn in the casket with her mother.

I did as I was told and ran my ring finger across her hair. A sweet peace came over me. "Rest, Momma. No one will ever replace you, but your babies are going to be OK."

She was absolutely stunning. Thirty-three years old. We were told by an old classmate that she was one of the sweetest girls you'd ever meet in high school. Against all odds, she became a high school graduate with two babies, and then she fell into a life any of us could fall into, given the right circumstances.

I watched these babies hold each other that day—Big Sis, her boyfriend, Big Brother, Elizabeth, James, and Michelle—right in that funeral room. The grief was like a weighted blanket: heavy but comfortable.

Gah, I don't think I'd ever been so proud of a group of kids who didn't share my DNA. Not one of them has hit the ripe old age of twenty as I write this, and each of them had the strength of a seventy-year-old combat veteran that day. I'm convinced God makes these children of trauma out of the toughest steel that heaven has to offer.

I've said it before and I'll say it again. I could've left this planet with utter joy that very day, seeing that God carries forth what the enemy decimates. It was so incredibly powerful.

Chapter 11

We Are Connected

Right now, I feel very compelled to bring the reader back to the first few chapters of this book.

"K" (we'll call her), my bonus babies' thirty-three-year-old mom of five, died knowing that her children had found new parents, new brothers and sisters, new purposes, new activities, and new comforts. I'm sure that in her heart, she felt she had fully lost them.

After months of moving forward, she lost her battle quickly and abruptly. Her death was tragic.

When I was thirty-three years old, I wanted to die. I wholeheartedly believed I wasn't enough and that my children deserved better. I believed that my death would propel Ryan into meeting a new wife and give him a new start with more babies. I believed my whole household would function better without me.

Our Savior, Jesus Christ, died at thirty-three, so that both K and I could live a life of abundance, freedom, and joy.

I live in West Virginia. There is quite a bit of controversy in this state over the origin of our addiction, mental health, poverty, and foster care problems and how to solve them.

But let me tell you what Momma K, without ever meeting her, taught me about life in general.

Addicts don't make little baby addicts. It's not that simple.

Narcissists don't casually make baby narcissists.

Those with bipolar disorder don't raise up manic-depressive children.

The single most important factor for addiction, bipolar disorder, OCD, anxiety, and depression in a child is at least some sort of consistent abuse.

I'm not talking about a smack on the bottom or yelling every once in a while when a child is being defiant and we're struggling with our emotions. At that point, we've traded in the real debate for a lightweight one.

I'm talking about when the parents' mental state causes them to psychologically, verbally, emotionally, physically, and sexually abuse their child consistently without any regard for what they're doing.

Is it possible to understand that most mentally ill, abusive homes have a plethora of these abuses? Therefore, the outcome is always the same. The child is always made to feel no good, worthless, dispensable, and even invisible.

Guess what. I used that word today before I opened up my laptop.

I said, "I feel invisible."

Mommas, how we were raised, the words that were said to us, the bitters that we carry on our backs, the chips on our shoulders—these things have to be brought to the Light.

Further, when we look at women like Momma K or others who are struggling to be upstanding citizens, what if we began to see ourselves in them?

I remember a time very early in having the babies. I was so miffed with their momma. I couldn't imagine how anything in this world could win over those precious kids.

But now I see it differently.

Hopelessness.

Momma, have you ever felt that? I did tonight actually.

There's more than one abuser in my life. There's a lot more narcissistic people walking around in general. They have a lot of people fooled.

I have very guarded relationships with them because of their psychological and manipulative abuse.

But I watch them. We live in the same little area of life. I have to interact with them sometimes.

There're days where I am so triggered by their gas lighting that I feel like a caged animal.

I can't help but wonder if or how long K felt like that before she gave into the lies of the enemy and her struggles for the last time.

I wonder how often K was reminded that she was nothing or called back to a story from who she used to be, reminded of all the things that she'd never get to do with her kids.

Oh, time with their momma may have been ten years away because of the court's decisions, but the kids and I had plans. They loved her. We prayed for her.

Momma, please hear this over the roar of the enemy.

Keep going.

Let me tell you something. No matter how you decide to feed your babies, bed your babies, play with your babies, and the like, not one preteen, adolescent, or adult child is going to care about what you did back then.

"Does Mom love me *today?* Does she cherish me *today?* Does she consider me a blessing *today?*"

Whether you're like me and get to homeschool your babies and have the chance to speak life into them daily or a mom who's waiting on being reunited with her child due to some past choices, we are all Mom.

All that my babies have are vague memories and the promise from Mom, Dad, aunts, cousins, brothers, and sisters that K loved them.

I cannot and do not want to leave them. She left me as the one who cannot break their heart, and I will do all I can to not disappoint her, even on the hard days.

I've been given an incredible gift.

Chapter 12

The Present

As I write this, it's been six months since my bonus babies' biological mother passed away. I'm pretty sure taking them to her funeral was the best and worst choice we've made thus far.

The behaviors have come out. The littles are still grasping the fact that they didn't come from my tummy the way three of their older siblings did and that they share the same "tummy" Mommy with two siblings they only periodically see. They're all still reeling from the finality and surreal nature of what they've gone through. She was a woman they barely knew but who was connected to them in a way deeper than any other human being on the planet.

Despite this, I could never live with myself if I had kept them home on that sunny morning in May. They deserved closure. It will mean more later than now. Yet it gives back just a little piece of what was taken from all three of them.

Adoption is painful and hard for everyone. I've heard it

described on several occasions as a "broken hallelujah," and I think that is so profound.

Adoption means leaving a child with unanswered questions, rejections, wondering why they weren't good enough to keep or fight for, and always analyzing whether they are truly worthy of love.

However, adoption can also mean redemption. Growing past previous anger and hurt into something beautiful. It can mean using what happened to you (some of the worst trauma imaginable) to be a light for others.

With my comorbidities in the area of mental health and trauma, my struggles with mom guilt, grief, and the choice to homeschool, I oftentimes wonder still if I'm doing all six of my kids more harm than good.

Listen. I still lose it some days.

Here's what I believe God says to me through the enemy's lies: "You are Mine. You are loved. You are learning."

We are inundated with research about the first one thousand days of life, and boy, are those days important. The younger a child is, the more flexible the brain. But new research says that those neuropathways (we'll talk more about that later) can change course well into adulthood. And *this* is good news and the grace of a loving God.

Momma, we don't have to be perfect or fear screwing it all up. How much more can a child learn from a parent when they watch them learn and grow as well?

Let them see your tears. Let them watch you mess up. Let

them hear your apology. Let them watch you heal. Let them be a witness to your cycle breaking.

Feel the weight of the guilt and conviction of your anger when it's directed toward your little ones, and then give it to God and ask for your baby's forgiveness.

I don't know this for a fact because my children aren't there yet, but I have a theory.

If I do all this, I will probably still hear the words "Mom, it was hurtful when you used to (fill in the blank)" one day.

My prayer is that on that day, I will be able to say with complete peace, "I am so sorry I hurt you. I don't have an excuse. I failed you that day, those weeks, those years, and I ask you and the Lord for forgiveness."

This is real growth.

We can go on any social media outlet and find all the ways society says that we are screwing up our kids.

God's Word warns of children being completely disobedient and defiant of their parents' teachings, and we are witnessing a generation of children who are being taught that their parents are bigoted and wrong on every point.

The only thing we have to fight with is the humility and love of Christ.

The only choice we have is truth and light.

The truth of God's Word.

The light to shine in the dark places, even our own.

Part 2

What I've Learned about This Broken World and the Grace of God

Chapter 13

Childhood Trauma

(How Common, Tragic, and
Underplayed It Truly Is)

I don't have a degree in psychology, psychiatry, or even counseling. However, I do have experience with adults and children who've dealt with trauma, namely myself.

First and foremost, there is something that we don't say enough and that many weary mommas need to hear. Are you ready for this?

We *all* traumatize our kids sometimes.

Sin is part of this world's landscape. The fall has rendered us incapable of always being on top of our emotions, living in the Spirit 100 percent of the time, or batting a thousand. Biblical shame over our poor choices and sin when it comes to everything (including mistreating or hurting our kids) is a good thing, but we can't live there.

My reason for the title of this book is twofold. While I feel like the words "Get up" from the Lord saved my life, I also think it's what He's commanding us moms to do every day despite how we may feel about ourselves.

For decades, the word *abuse* was oversimplified. We now know that there are many of us out there who suffered under consistent messages and lies about the core of who we are.

We have two choices. We can either ignore, stuff down, and self-medicate our traumas *or* we can face and heal them.

I suggest for anyone who thinks they may somehow be traumatized to take the ACE (adverse childhood experiences) survey.[2] It is simple, straightforward, and helpful. All the information is on the CDC's web site. (I scored a 3.)

This study has revealed that around half of adults have most likely experienced significant trauma in their childhood (rewiring neuropathways in the brain, causing emotional and physical signs and symptoms), and the majority of us have experienced at least something that has caused an adverse reaction.

The works of Marcus Warner,[3] Dr. Neil Anderson,[4] and others have also been of major help to me and add to this concept in my opinion. Satan speaks lies into our core when we are vulnerable and traumatized. We internalize those lies, and they became the main ways that we see ourselves. If we don't replace those lies with

---

[2] "Violence Prevention: Adverse Childhood Experiences," CDC, www.cdc.gov/violenceprevention/aces/index.html.

[3] Dr. Marcus Warner's most influential book for me has been *Understanding the Wounded Heart* (Deeper Walk International, 2020).

[4] Dr. Neil Anderson's most influential book for me has been *Victory of the Darkness* (Bethany House Publishers, revised and updated July 2020).

reminders of who we are in Christ, we will pass them down to the next generation. If we *do* replace them, we've not only successfully rewired our own neuropathways (pretty stinking cool), but we've also become cycle breakers in a very permanent, lasting way.

So what do we do when we know that we haven't batted a thousand in our parenting?

We do what we do/did when we accepted Christ as our Savior and continually repent. We acknowledge to our children our bad choices, apologize, ask for forgiveness, and turn from our sinful, selfish ways. Also, we return them to joy by smiling, hugging, loving, and tickling face-to-face, eyeball-to-eyeball, and heart-to-heart.

I need the reader to hear what I'm saying. It is *not* OK for a parent to consistently maltreat a child with fists, put-downs, withholding food or other basic needs, neglect, etc. This is why I have three adopted children and why child protective services exist.

However, if we sin against each other, it's only logical that we'll sin against our children. They're humans too, and we need their forgiveness as well.

In the next chapters, I'll be discussing cultural issues and concerns. These all, I believe, find their start in trauma.

Chapter 14

The Intricate Details of Cycle Breaking

The Lord passed before him and proclaimed, "The
Lord, the Lord, a God merciful and gracious,
slow to anger and abounding in steadfast love and
faithfulness, keeping steadfast love for thousands,
forgiving iniquity and transgression and sin, but who
will by no means clear the guilty, visiting the iniquity
of the fathers on the children and the children's
children, to the third and the fourth generation."

—Exodus 34:6–7[5]

Before diving into what I believe it looks like to do the hard yet
somewhat trending work of cycle breaking, I feel I need to be
clear. I'm not a biblical scholar or a therapist. However, I'm sure
you've learned by now that I've been through some things.

---

[5] The Holy Bible, ESV Study, Crossway, 2008.

So as long as you envision us at a coffee shop or playground during this chapter and not a big, gray office, I think this will go well.

The Bible makes it clear that we all have sinned and fallen short. There's not one of us who is 100 percent clear of traumas, bondages, and strongholds.

When I look at Exodus 34:6–7, here's what I think the Holy Spirit is conveying to me:

There have been many, *many* wicked generations since the beginning of time. Some families have thrown their hands up and allowed the enemy to crush them without any kind of fight. Other families have lived in denial and covered their skeleton-filled closet with the latest trends, "right ways," and modern verbiage.

It is rare and beautiful, however, for God to find a family, usually prompted by the soft, weary heart of a momma, that says, "Lord, forgive us. Keep us close. Comfort us when we sin. Journey with us. Expose our dark and Your light for our good and Your glory.

You see, if you were hurt as a child and then continued to hurt your children in the same or different ways without a second thought, God isn't causing this. He's simply visiting it.

He's peeping in to see if you might become convicted of your pain. He's not just concerned about your kids but you as well.

He's checking in to see if you might want Him to heal your heart and to turn away from all the things that hurt you when you were small. If you turn to Him, He will begin to forgive and heal. You will still make mistakes, and you'll still somehow "traumatize" your child. We all do in one way or another. This is mostly because we're not always aware of our own triggers—much less those of our children.

However, you'll learn to parent not from guilt but joy. You'll learn to let go of the bad days and celebrate the good. You'll learn how deep a child's love is for their parent or parents and how deep the Father's love is for all of us.

I'm sure you've heard it said that an abused child either repeats the cycle of their parents or the exact opposite. Both of these are trauma responses, and God wants neither. Our children were meant to refine us and teach us. They are meant, in part, to be the catalyst that encourages healing. I would implore you to see your weaknesses in your relationship with your child and seek help if you've suffered trauma. There's nothing more beautiful than a family healing together and the impact that it makes on a child who can say, "I remember when God healed my mom."

Chapter 15

The Toxic "Perfect Mom" Culture

If there is one thing I am deeply concerned about, it is how this generation of children is going to turn out emotionally as adults raised by social media-traumatized moms.

So here it is. Plain and simple. Write these words all over your house, mommas young and old! What you feed your child (as long as it's meant to be edible), how you birth your child, where you send your child to school, where your baby sleeps, how many children you have, whether or not you vaccinate, and whether you stay inside the home or work outside it are *not* sin versus obedience issues. *None of them.*

I encourage any woman who suffers with false guilt to visit www.gotquestions.org. It is a foundationally solid, Bible-based web site that answers questions like "Is it sinful to have an epidural?" and "Is it OK to use formula?" with grace and truth.

For some of you, especially in the older generations, these

seem like silly questions. However, I know where my girls are. The younger crowd is hurting—and dying—over these things.

To add to this point, one of these decisions over the other *does not* add spirituality or maturity to a woman's life. Obedience to Christ does. Period.

Please don't compare the way you conduct your household to others. There are many "Christian" households who have unknowingly begun to follow new age, secular practices in their parenting.

"Scientific research" has become extremely biased and flat-out wrong in many areas. This is due to the payout that scientific breakthroughs receive. It has influenced even the people we should be able to completely trust, such as doctors, caretakers, authors, and mental health professionals.

Other ways moms have fallen into legalistic, pseudo-Christian traps have been through extreme conservatism, spiritual progressivism, moneymaking corporations targeting motherhood, and frankly, bots posing as real people on social media.

One of my favorite verses has become 1 Thessalonians 4:11–12 (ESV). "And to aspire to live quietly, and to mind your own affairs, and to work with your hands, as we instructed you, so that you may walk properly before outsiders and be dependent on no one."

This verse reminds me to unplug and to be unbothered by the decisions of others and how they feel about mine. The job of my husband and me is to raise our children "in the discipline and instruction of the Lord" (Ephesians 6:4[6]) and to encourage

---

[6] The Holy Bible, ESV Study, Crossway, 2008.

other Christian mothers to do the same. I'm not to advise them on feeding, birthing, etc. unless they ask for it or they are directly harming their child (which isn't a very common occurrence).

However, I will forever and always reassure mothers that these insignificant choices (in the long run) are OK no matter what and that they have to do what is best for their household and mental, emotional, and physical stability.

Lastly, what I want to scream to this toxic mom culture is to *please* let the dad be dad (a.k.a., an equal coparent). Obviously, I understand that there are circumstances where Dad is not or cannot be in the picture, but it's hard to underplay the role of a father in a child's life.

This toxic mom culture is telling us we have to do it all, and it is creating crippling problems for our children. They need father roles in their lives. Our daughters need a healthy man to affirm their beauty and identity, and our sons need a sensitive, masculine figure to exemplify what true strength looks like. Do not steal these gifts from them, Momma. Let them lead. Let them nurture. Above all, let them give you a break!

One of the most redemptive and correspondingly condemning things about our modern culture is the many ways that we can be a godly family without fitting into past or present cultural norms. Of course, it is still lovely for Mom to stay home with the children, but she can now become a life-saving doctor or an empowering teacher. Dad can stay home with the kids and still be the leader while Mom works and supports the family financially.

Even though Ryan and I have more traditional roles now, we've been all over the place in the past. I am blessed to have a true, godly partner who actually leads our home and assists in nurturing our children. We aren't meant to do it alone.

Even with Ryan and me tag-teaming hard every single day, it's still overwhelming. Not having family close or anyone who is sold-out committed to our tribe means that we do 98 percent of the work with no extended support. This isn't how it should be, but it's what so many families face.

In this toxic mom culture, let's give each other grace, encouragement, and love. Let's make choices based on what's best for the needs of our family and not what will make us look the most praiseworthy.

Chapter 16

Autonomy, Abortion, and the LGBTQ+ Movement

Autonomy is "the quality or state of self-governing" (Oxford Languages).[7]

To be honest, there are ways that I'm completely behind the idea that we are in charge when it comes to decisions about our own bodies.

You would be hard-pressed to find a mother who will more enthusiastically than I approve her daughters' violent acts when/ if a boy lays an unwanted hand, foot, mouth, etc. on her body.

My kids are allowed to have whatever haircut they want.

I am not a stickler for particular clothes and shoes on any given occasion.

---

[7] "Autonomy," *Oxford Languages.*

I chuckle to myself when my kids dress up as each other (even across gender) for kicks and giggles.

However, we as parents have also made a lot of decisions about their minds and bodies. Some of those that push bodily autonomy would most likely gasp at some of the things we have "forced upon" our children, but the Bible instructs children to obey parents and parents to instruct, care for, and "govern" their children.

Out of abuse, trauma, and even entitlement, there has birthed a movement within our young adults that says they can do whatever they want with their own bodies and can hand these ideals down to their very small children.

Let me make something perfectly clear. In our country where hundreds, if not thousands, of self-proclaiming "Christian" families are torn apart by narcissism, adultery, domestic abuse, sexual abuse, and the like, it doesn't surprise me that we are here.

I've learned from my own journey that the solution to childhood trauma is never to rebel, and a rough childhood is no excuse for exposing children to ideas and truths beyond their care, comprehension, or processing.

We must look within ourselves first.

Homosexuality, bisexuality, polygamy, polyamory, transgenderism, abortion, and the like have been around almost as long as humankind. As much as we would all like to think that there is a particular "something" in childhood or adolescence that forms these thought processes, there's really not much scientifically to back that up.

We are all prone to biological and psychological abnormalities, and let's be honest. Sin, as the Bible defines, can be a lot of fun, exhilarating, and self-gratifying for a time.

For generations, children have been told that adults are always right, that their feelings are not valid, and that they simply must obey their parents because that's how it is. We've neglected the goodness of God—His favor, His blessing, and His peace. We've neglected giving our kids even the least bit of redemptive autonomy to figure out who they are for His glory.

Due to this negligence, there is now a generation of young people who are bitter and angry. Most of these adults were never able to meet the expectations of parents who felt they did everything right and that their kids lost their way. These adult children have now decided to set new standards for themselves that are counter to everything they were taught. They are redefining their gender, experimenting sexually in harmful ways, and promoting (as well as participating in) the killing of babies all for the sake of "my body, my choice."

This pendulum swing is dangerous and really clear right now in the chaos of our world.

But friend, let me tell you there's always hope.

When we return to the Gospel, when we die to ourselves and our own narrow perspectives, when we ask the Holy Spirit to show us the hearts of those we love and pray for, He can make such a difference.

If your child has, is in the middle of, or is heading into these cultural struggles, continue to love them. We are to preach the truth in love, even and especially to our own biological and adopted offspring. We are to hear their hearts and then shine the

Gospel in those darkened places. We are to show through our own lives what it looks like to humble our hearts, souls, minds, and bodies in submission to our Creator and Savior.

We are to have a redemptive, Christ-honoring, "me too" movement within our homes.

Chapter 17

Redefining a Healthy, Christian Marriage

I want to start this chapter by saying that I have witnessed single, Christian mothers and fathers raising their children to be amazing young adults who love Christ fiercely. Although I believe that a traditional, loving, Christlike marriage is the healthiest for a child's well-being, we live in a sin-filled broken world and this is not always possible.

My husband and I have moved so far away from where we used to be on this subject, and I feel like it was just in time for him to accept a position as senior pastor of a church as God tossed struggling couples our way.

The American Christian culture for decades has spoken about divorce in a very narrow, rigid narrative. The church has not honored the gray or the individual complexity of each couple's struggles.

There are a couple of verses that stand out to me as I write about divorce in this chapter.

- 1 Corinthians 7:15 – "But if the unbelieving partner separates, let it be so. In such cases the brother or sister is not enslaved. God has called you to peace."[8]
- Matthew 19:9 – "And I say to you: whoever divorces his wife, except for sexual immorality, and marries another, commits adultery."[9]

I won't spend much time on the latter.

Adultery, stepping outside the marriage for another sexual relationship, is grounds for divorce for the one who has been offended no matter the gender. Christians have known and believed this for a long time. Some have chosen to stay in a relationship tainted by adultery and work toward a repentant and reconciled marriage. This is admirable in many cases. In others, it becomes futile as the offending party doesn't ever seem to change.

However, 1 Corinthians 7:15 is a little more complex and has been read for far too long as, basically, "If they leave, let 'em leave." I believe it's far more intricate than that.

Although much of our "internet enlightenment" in the last few decades has been harmful, many destructive things psychologically and spiritually within marriage have also been revealed that need the church's attention.

The 1 Corinthians verse can be interpreted multiple ways,

---

[8] The Holy Bible, ESV Study, Crossway, 2008.
[9] The Holy Bible, ESV Study, Crossway, 2008.

but here's my sincere belief. If a man or woman is consistently and continuously abusing their partner physically, verbally, mentally, and/or spiritually without true repentance or change, they are showing themselves to not only be unbelievers but to have abandoned or separated emotionally from marriage.

In my opinion, this includes narcissistic abuse and the abuse of patriarchal or "headship" titles. The destruction firsthand I've seen bestowed upon the children of these marriages is truly unreal. Many seem to spend the majority of their lives in an altered reality from those brothers and sisters living out their faith right alongside them. They never connect. They never understand real relationships. To put it mildly, their attachment is frayed.

If you read the marriage verses in the book of Ephesians (5:22–33) in context, they really are beautiful.

In almost twenty years of marriage, my husband has never made a decision for our family that I've adamantly opposed. Why not? Because he trusts me and knows that if I'm consistently in opposition to something, the Holy Spirit is communicating wrong timing on his part at the very least.

In almost twenty years of marriage, I've allowed my husband to make many decisions for our family without very much discussion. Why? Because I trust that he is following the guidance of the Holy Spirit.

While I do not condone leaving a marriage at the first sign of opposition and I very much encourage counseling and trying to save "Christian" marriages to a point, I also think it simply doesn't work when one partner is not willing to humble themselves for the joy and spiritual health of the other. Towing the line spiritually for another person, much less an entire family, is a burden Christ never intended for us to carry on our own. It never grants the peace to which God has called us.

I would encourage all couples to treat each other the way Christ has treated and pursued them. This is and always will be a beautiful, powerful example for your children. Maybe this sounds a bit oversimplified, but it holds so much truth.

Momma, if you are in a relationship where you've tried what feels like everything (counseling, loving confrontation, going to the pastor or elders of your church, etc.) and you're living in a space where you feel belittled, hurt, demeaned, gaslit, manipulated, and/or personally assaulted, you do not have to live like this. God does not say that you do. Staying together for the sake of the children is not worth it if their male role model is no example for them at all.

Follow the guidance of the Holy Spirit. Pray and have others you trust pray. Then don't wait until your life is half over and you and your children have lived through years of trauma to find a way to let go.

I have seen people experience healing from narcissism and selfishness, but more often than not, this comes after their other half has put their foot down, set boundaries, and sometimes walked completely away.

Whether you and your spouse exemplify a godly marriage or you were brave enough to walk away from an abusive one, you're setting an example for your children that the Lord will bless.

Chapter 18

An Unending List of False Gods

Momma, I've got some bad news. We live in a culture that in no way perpetuates the Gospel. That wellness guru you follow, those tips on gentle parenting, that family of eighteen who has their own cable show—they are almost all governed by a worldview that is not centered in the truth.

The reality is that a huge part of seemingly Christian culture isn't centered around the truth.

Scripture makes clear that anything we do is meaningless unless it's meant to draw us close to our God. All this added stuff that we've thrown on our plate may look good on the surface, but in this culture, it's taking the place of our relationship with Jesus.

A woman can be letting her diet go, feeding her kids McDonald's regularly, and having an unkempt house and still be drawing ever closer to God. She can also be eating nothing but kale, making all of her children's meals from scratch, and having a dazzling house and still be in total bondage to the enemy.

Our outward appearance has very little to do with what's going on inside. We worship so many things other than God.

I discovered my joy through dropping out of the world's perfectionist race. I've learned (and am still learning) to find my joy in Jesus. My house doesn't look like you could eat off the floors, our main bathroom constantly has toothpaste gobs all over it, Wendy's four-for-four meals become a staple in our family during sports seasons, my girls' hair gets tangles, and the boys' room oftentimes smells like, well, boys.

I've also learned that worshipping my children only brings me grief and sets the bar of expectation way too high. The more I love them the way God made them, lead and talk to them about Jesus, and ask for forgiveness when I slip up, the more I see them turn their faces toward Him. Every Sunday that they wear what they feel comfortable into worship, every sports game we leave where simply "Good job today!" is spoken, and every time I let go a little, I see them running into my arms and the faith that they've inherited.

Mommas, you don't have to control everything. You don't have to sacrifice yourselves at the altar of inspiration, and you don't have to kill yourself to be considered enough.

Our Christian culture has for centuries absorbed all that is "popular" and "looks good" in secular culture and adapted and added it to the Gospel. Within the church, these adaptations and additions many times become topics of conversation, then encouragement, then an unspoken new law, then an idol. Before we know it, the homeschooling mom with ten kids and a side hustle holds more value than the mom of one in public school struggling to hold down a job in her line of work. We make these judgments about one another and within ourselves, and the outcome is devastating.

Today, I admittedly went down one of these unending "rabbit trails" of social media. (If ya know, ya know.) I happened upon a sweet momma's page who had experienced a successful home birth with her first child. (This is something I never fathomed when having my children, and I find myself intrigued yet a bit frightened by it.)

This mother was clearly a self-identified Christian and made even her birthing experience a beautiful worship experience. What concerned me was that in a later post, she stated that she was trying to find a group of "like-minded" mothers.

She was not referring to the Gospel.

She was referring to birthing and rearing choices.

In a way, I get it. I feel much more comfortable with my friends who took that epidural or C-section, vaxxed those kids, and used a healthy mixture of breastmilk and formula when it was what was best for their family.

But when I fall into that, I'm idolizing.

The truth is that those who made very different choices from me, put the Gospel first, and love the Lord above everything else make the best of friends.

Why?

Because we share the priority of the Holy Spirit, the kindness of Christ, and the unconditional love of the Father.

We see and appreciate each other's parenting successes and woes because the Gospel means failing and relying on Christ's redemption again and again and again.

We *truly* see each other as beloved sisters in Christ made in the image of our divine Father.

Chapter 19

How God's Word Aligns with Hopeful Brain Research

(and Why the Internet Isn't Hopeful at All)

Weary Momma, I don't know about you, but my heart breaks over all the physical, emotional, mental, and spiritual issues our young ones face. We've been blessed with six kids whose sensory and attention deficit problems are mild comparatively, so I'm treading lightly on this topic because I know many who struggle so deeply.

This week while taking a break from writing, I went all over the internet asking particular questions. I realized that to find what I was looking for, namely a secular hope, I had to be very specific in my wording.

See, when we notice our children struggling (or maybe we don't and we're just questioning if a decision will cause future struggling—'cuz we can be a bit neurotic), we as mothers are quick to self-blame. Could it have been our diet when we were pregnant? What about those couple times we *really* lost our temper? Too much TV? Too much McDonald's? Should we have homeschooled so they could've avoided that bully or questionable teacher altogether?

However, the Gospel confirms that in fact, God's Sovereignty is 100 percent. He is in complete control and our children are where He wants them to be.

It has taken me a long time to pick this concept up, and sometimes I still drop it. I'm type A at heart. I'm really good at blaming myself for things beyond my control and knowledge. Faith is hard for me because facts are more comfortable and reassuring. I'm not proud of this, but I know I'm a work in progress and God hasn't given up on me.

Here though is the maddening piece. Did you know if you ask the right questions on the internet, it has to give itself away?

Question: How much of our current scientific research is false?

Answer:

> The study in Science Advances is the latest to highlight the "replication crisis" where results, mostly in social science and medicine, fail to hold up when other researchers try to repeat experiments. Following an influential paper in 2005 titled Why most published research findings are false, three major projects have found

replication rates as low as 39% in psychology journals, 61% in economics journals, and 62% in social science studies published in the Nature and Science, two of the most prestigious journals in the world." *(The Guardian, 2021[10])*

Let's try again.

Question: When do children's brains stop developing? Answer:

Though the brain may be done growing in size, it does not finish developing and maturing until the mid- to late 20s. The front part of the brain, called the prefrontal cortex, is one of the last brain regions to mature." ("7 Things to Know about the Teen Brain," NIMH[11])

Over the course of several years, I've done my own quick dives into neuroplasticity research, and it is incredible. Momma, there is *always* hope. Give yourself grace.

Maybe you were in a high-stress situation when your kids

---

[10] Ian Sample, "Research Findings That Are Probably Wrong Cited Far More than Robust Ones, Study Finds," *The Guardian,* https://www.theguardian.com/science/2021/may/21/research-findings-that-are-probably-wrong-cited-far-more-than-robust-ones-study-finds, 2021 (27-10-22).

[11] "Seven Things to Know about the Teen Brain," National Institute of Mental Health, Bethesda, MD, US Department of Health and Human Services, National Institutes of Health, *https://www.nimh.nih.gov/health/publications/the-teen-brain-7-things-to-know*, 2020 (27-10-2022).

were little and look back on those years with regret and remorse. Maybe you did great back then, but these middle or teen years are killing you.

We have discovered that although those first one thousand days are pretty important, there is still abounding hope. Our brains and our children's brains are amazingly resilient and open to the hard work of those who love them unconditionally.

Also, and maybe a little more humbling, those of us who strive for some unattainable perfection may find ourselves at the end of our parenting adventure as the older child in the story of the prodigal son. The reward for parenting our children well every day is that we parented them well every day. The end.

The party and the fattened calf will be left for the struggler, the one who has walked through the fire, learned some things the hard way, and found Christ residing in their child and themselves.

Miracles happen when we hope. When we trust God. When we keep fighting for the child, we feel like maybe we've somehow damaged.

The internet, our culture, the pagan world wants us to be fearful and to crave the popular, "correct," more self-martyring choice. That's what makes the money. That's what helps with bias.

Please know, dear sister, that when you are prayerful, when you trust who truly holds your children, when you rest yourself and your children in His loving care, He is blessing you in ways yet to be revealed. Unlike all of us, He is a good, perfect Father.

If He loves you, your idols will fall. This isn't to punish you but to peel back the scales on your eyes so that You can see Him more clearly.

Epilogue

If you just finished reading this little book, I would ask you to do one thing for me.

Don't ever doubt your love for your family or desire to know God.

Mothers who have a narcissistic or unhealthy version of "love" for their children don't care to read books like this. Mothers who care are those who do their best with what they know, and this could look so vastly different for every individual in a world with so many options. There is not one "sinless" way for spouses to start and raise a family.

Yes, there's sin that we all commit. Some are even more prevalent in females: jealousy, gossip, comparison, bitterness, malice, a rebellious spirit, etc.

The saddest part is that we do much more confronting and questioning over the nonessentials than we do holding one another accountable in love for true sins and struggles.

I desire to be reminded more often that I need to check my

spirit of bitterness or my tendency to compare. I would much rather be biblically, lovingly "shamed" over the things that matter than I would over what I fed or how I disciplined my child.

Sweet sister, wouldn't you?

What if we ignored the things that don't matter and instead checked each other's spirits and walked with each other lovingly through the things that do?

What if instead of seeing life as a race against each other, we saw it as encouraging onward until we meet Jesus face-to-face.

The Bible promises us that anything we do as followers of Christ for our own accolades will fall, and He has proven that to me over and over.

Oh, how He must love me, because everything I attempt on my own fails miserably.

Does that resonate with you?

My deepest prayer is that this book changes our vision and that we stop looking to the things of this world to ensure bright, healthy families and simply trust in our source of joy.

Dear friend, thank you for reading. I am praying for you.

My Prayer for Every Woman (Including Myself)

Lord, please remind all women who know You that *nothing* can ever separate them from Your love. The powers of darkness are raging in our culture and the battle for the mind seems impossible to win. I know.

Father, we mommas aren't strangers to the demons that have held us in bondage for a long time, especially perfectionism and defeat. Our souls have been wrestling long and hard with these demons. They don't care if they contradict themselves, as long as they keep us in fear and confusion.

The dark depth of the internet and the ways the powers of the dark use it to toss hate, calamity, name-calling, comparison, and perfectionism around like rag dolls can leave us so weary. We have a front row seat to everyone's highlight reel and the enemy has a field day with that.

We are drowning in the lies of the enemy. We are missing the fullness of Your love and joy today because it's hard not to trip over the accusations of the condemner.

Lord, show us how to look past family and cultural practices, to ignore the venomous snakes in the fields of birthing, rearing, and parenting. Help us to be encouragers.

We believe, Lord, that these dark spirits will flee when they see the joy rising out of us, the desire and trust we have that the shadow of Your wings will be our resting place.

We know You will heal us in time, and it starts now. We will do all we can to fix our eyes on You.

In our Savior's name, amen.

The Gospel

Momma, if this book has been refreshing yet intriguing and/or confusing to you and you're not sure you know the true Gospel, let me take a second to tell you about it.

God created a perfect world, but He knew it wouldn't last. In the first generation (Adam and Eve), sin (bad choices and bad outcomes) entered the world. This sin separated us from a God who walked among us in the beginning.

Through centuries, sin broke the world. The Bible talks about events like Noah's ark and King David's multiple sins that exemplify this deep, dark, hopeless state in which we all are living.

God, being a loving Father over His creation, sent His Son, Jesus, into the world. Jesus lived perfectly, died a criminal's death, and defeated the grave so that those who are/were called could be reunited with our Creator for eternity. He sends all believers the Holy Spirit, the third person of Himself (along with the Father and Son), to guide all followers and live within us.

We now live in a world still rattled with generational sin,

disease, immorality, greed, and all sorts of evil. God's enemy, the devil, creates and encourages these pitfalls. We even partake in them at times. However, thanks be to God and the sacrifice of His Son, we are seen as perfect sons and daughters of the King and have a place in heaven. As we walk in our new life with Christ, we fall sometimes, but the Holy Spirit, through sanctification, convicts us and heals through prayer, Bible study, and the support of the local church.

If you believe this message and don't know where to turn next, you can always message me on FB @thegraceofgettingup.

Acknowledgments

There are so many people I have to thank for the writing of this book.

If you're reading this and ever encouraged me to write a book, thank you so much. I wrote "for free" for years, and so many people were loyally reading, encouraging, and helping me see my gift.

I'm so thankful to my husband in this process. We have six kids with a lot of needs, but he never failed to allow me to retreat and write. I only stayed up way past my bedtime a couple of times to work on this project.

My two older kids, Cohen and Ella, were so excited for me to become an official author. They have seen the best and worst of me and had nothing but good things to say about my choosing to finally let out my story in writing. I'm thankful to Ella for her beautiful artwork on the cover.

Robert J. Day of Patrick Henry Services (Brookneal, West Virginia) is the author of a three-part series on his own life growing up in and out of foster care and the struggles he faced as an adult. He was my boss for two years and one of the best there ever was or will be. He took the time in his busy schedule to set up a Zoom meeting with me and lead me through the beginning of this book. He and his lovely wife, Karen, also took the time to read over the rough draft.

I am thankful to my bonus babies' big sister, Kenzie, who read all the deep, hard parts for me and approved them so I made sure I honored two families, not just one. She deserves all the good the world has to offer and we love her so.

I had so many "Momma readers and encouragers" when I was working on this project. Some of the most helpful were my friends Karie Farris, Lindsay Burdett, Tara Kitchen, Jeanne Helmick, Barbara Kitchen, Candy Payne, Katie Powell (another published author), Morgan Stow, Sarah Wills Akers, Amy Kirk, and so many other prayer warriors and gatekeepers.

Thank you for your contributions, prayers, and cheerleading.

In the middle of writing this book, I began submitting articles to *Her View from Home* at herviewfromhome.com. They have published everything I've written for them and served as a confidence booster as well as a great help in promoting this book. If you're a mom of any age feeling the call to write, I encourage you to submit a piece and join their team. They are the only constantly positive, amazingly encouraging social media team I've ever come across.

Ultimately, I'd like to thank my Savior, Jesus Christ. Without Him, there would be no story. I'll talk about what He's done in my life any day of the week.

About the Author

Crystal Fulmer is a pastor's wife and homeschooling mom to 6 kids; some grew in her womb and some in her heart. God is sanctifying her through anxiety, depression, OCD, and personal trauma as well as trauma care. She has a Master's in Education and has worked in private schools, public schools, and group home settings. An advocate for removing mental illness stigma, combating toxic supermom culture, foster care, and adoption, she is passionate about writing that will minister to others. Through this medium, her ultimate goal is to use her experiences enriched by the Word of God to glorify Christ and the Gospel message. She resides in Cross Lanes, WV with her husband, 6 children, 2 cats, and 2 dogs. Her favorite place to be in life is with her family; preferably by the ocean or in a cabin in the mountains. She is a classic introvert and loves all things peace-giving. You are welcome into her community @thegraceofgettingup on Facebook or Instagram.